THOUGHTS INTO VERSES

Val Matthews Ashley

Pen Press

Copyright © Val Matthews Ashley 2009

All rights reserved

No part of this publication may be reproduced,
stored in a retrieval system, or transmitted
in any form or by any means, without
the prior permission in writing of the publisher,
nor be otherwise circulated in any form of binding or cover other
than that in which it is published and without a similar condition
including this condition being imposed on the subsequent
purchaser.

First published in Great Britain by Pen Press

All paper used in the printing of this book has been made from
wood grown in managed, sustainable forests.

ISBN13: 978-1-907172-34-2

Printed and bound in the UK
Pen Press is an imprint of Indepenpress Publishing Limited
25 Eastern Place
Brighton
BN2 1GJ

A catalogue record of this book is available from
the British Library

Cover design by Jacqueline Abromeit

Contents

Time	1
My Wish	2
Brother Love	3
Memories	4
Growing Old	5
Missing You	6
Nature's Own	7
Optimism	8
The Picture	9
My Mum	10
Melanie	11
Spalding	12
Keep A Candle Burning	13
Secrets	14
Over Sixty	15
Joe	16
Sweet Yesterday	17
I Believe	18
Peace	19
Woodthorpe Garden Centre	20
Little Jewels	21
Laughter	22
Colours	23
Isle Of Wight	24
A Walk Along The Sands	25
Alford	26
Wealth	27
Masters Of The Sky	28
Retirement	30
Our Heroes	31

Marmalade	32
The Auction	33
Woodhall Spa	34
One Lifetime	35
Circus	37
The Driving Test	38
Springtime	39
Dad	40
Flowers	41
Your Wedding	42
There's Always Me	43
Lincolnshire	44
If	45
My Wish	46
The Donkey	47
A Free Spirit	48
Happiness Is	49
Dreams	50
My Wish For You	51
Princess Diana	52
Charlie	53
Bertha	54
Henry	55
Remember Me	56
Friendship	57
The Written Word	58
The River	59
Courage	60
Christmas Time	61
The Way You Are	62
V.E. Day	63
Picnicking	64
Thinking Of You	65
Burma Star Heroes	66
Band Of Gold	67
Puddle Jumper	68

Tomorrow	69
Dear Santa	70
G.I. Joe	71
Alfred Lord Tennyson	72
An Illusive Dream	73
It's Your Day	74
I Know You	75
Maybe	76
You're Always There	77
Heather Lea	78
Days Like These	79
Titanic	80
Dad's Army	81
Together	82
Alford Craft Market	83
Thank You	84
The Gurkha	85
Floristry	86
One Moment Of Glory	87
A Little Thought	88
Funny Man	89
Sam	90
Barny	91
The Lone Sailors	92
Thoughts Of You	93
My Beloved Husband	94
ADMISSION 6d	95
A Little Dog Called Jack	96
Politics	97
James Mouse	98
The Flower Fairy	99
Martha's Birthday	101
Shed No Tears For Me	103
Ever The Optimist	104

Time

Time is a great healer so they say,
But the pain I felt when you died has never gone away,
Time passes, the seasons come and go,
I am left in a world I hardly know.
Time has slowed my step and lined my face,
But the love I feel inside for you, time will never erase,
Just as long as time is on my side,
I will hold my head up high, and walk with pride,
Time can be an enemy or a friend as well,
Especially when the tears inside me swell,
But time is for the living, the here and now,
So I must learn to smile again and get along somehow.

My Wish

If I had a wish fulfilled, it would surely be,
To set all impoverished people free,
Free from hunger, want and fear,
To fill their lives with hope and cheer,
To take away all their pain,
And watch them slowly smile again.
To do away with wars and strife,
Just let the people live their life,
Hopelessness is the thought that no one cares,
To let them know, someone hears,
I haven't much to offer, just simple words I know,
But from a tiny acorn, a giant oak will grow.

Brother Love

I used to sit upon your knee, in a time remembered long ago,
I took for granted you would be there, how could I really know,
That time was running out for you, life slowly ebbed away,
We watched it all happen, one awful August day.
You were so young, in fact just a boy,
Our parent's hearts were broken, you were their pride and joy.
No one moved the things you treasured, for what seemed years,
Every time Mum went in your room her eyes were filled with tears.
We can never know what the future would have held for you,
You were not given the chance to grow up, live your childhood through,
But you had already shown courage at such an early age,
Surely your name in gold is written upon that holy page.

Memories

We were inseparable, you and I,
In those balmy days gone by,
It's like a dream, when I think of it now,
So much fun and laughter, that's what I remember somehow.
The days were never long enough for the two of us then,
Tomorrow never bothered us, we didn't ask when.
The sun always seemed to shine, no cares or woes,
As we sat on the beach, the sand between our toes.
But of course this couldn't last, nothing ever does,
Your holiday over, I saw you to your bus.
I don't know where you came from, it must have been Heaven,
After all you were only six, but I was nearly seven.

Growing Old

I went to see my doctor, as I had something wrong with me,
I suppose I thought he would wave a magic wand, and set me free,
But life's not really like that, as I am sure you know quite well,
He listened very carefully to what I had to tell.
'Tests are needed in this case,' he said,
With brave face and beating heart I laid upon the bed.
Several weeks went by and then I had a letter,
Explaining what had to be done to make me feel better.
To help to cure all my ills,
The treatment was a load of pills.
That's alright, I can live with that,
It could be worse, I know where I'm at.
I'm grateful for all the years there's been nothing wrong with me,
But time has a way of catching up; it's called old age you see.

Missing You

It's so lonely now you're not here,
I keep looking at your empty chair.
It's all of two weeks since we were married in the church,
Now I feel abandoned, left in the lurch.
I don't know what to do now I have time to think,
Life was just a whirl, I didn't have time to blink.
It's the first time we've been apart since that happy day,
I didn't think it would affect me in quite this way.
I wish other women could give me a few tips,
Better make some tea, you'll be back soon with the fish
    and chips.

Nature's Own

Some beautiful flowers and majestic trees,
Burst forth as miracles from tiny seeds.
Corms and bulbs also play their part,
Producing such a display as to gladden the human heart.
The beauty of a landscape and the glory of the skies,
Cotton wool clouds drifting by inspires,
The artist to mimic Mother Nature's gown,
But no one can capture the wonder that's abound,
A bright silver moon hanging in the sky,
Black velvet background studded with diamonds on high.
A golden shining sun that warms all earth below,
How could anyone not believe in miracles I should like to know?
The ever-changing sea, the shifting sand,
The marvel that takes place by the unseen hand.
Are we so blind we cannot see nature's own rebirth,
The drama that is played out on our own precious earth.

Optimism

We must be optimistic in every thing we do,
We cannot let negative thoughts creep through,
Always look on the bright side and things will turn out well,
It may not be just when you want, but time alone will tell.
If the sun doesn't shine for you now, then tomorrow it
    certainly will,
So be positive in the knowledge that your dream you will fulfil.
So be grateful for the fact that you wake up every day,
Don't say it's boring; it doesn't have to be that way.
Start a new hobby, find interesting things to view,
Buy a lottery ticket, this time it could be you.

The Picture

I saw this gorgeous picture in your shop one day,
The fascination I had for it just wouldn't go away.
So when I had enough money I just had to buy it,
I hung it in my lounge where I can look and sit.
I often wondered if the scene was real,
If so where was it? It has such appeal.
A few years later I went on holiday to this lovely place,
We walked down the lane to the harbour and came face to face.
With this very scene we stepped into the picture and became part of it as well,
I now know its secret, but I'm not going to tell.

My Mum

She was an angel in disguise with auburn hair and blue-grey eyes,
She stood 5ft nothing in her stockinged feet,
Her heart was pure gold, and its every beat.
If she had something she thought you needed more than she,
Then it was yours, no question you see.
She only saw the good in others, no harm could she find,
It was a mortal blow to her when my brother Cyril died.
It was never destined she should live in this world very long,
She was like a brightly coloured bird who sang a brilliant song.
The day she fell asleep, as she would say,
The sun left the sky and all my world turned grey.
I've never said this before, I've bottled it up inside,
Because all of this happened when I was just a child.

Melanie

You were a little angel, so God thought he'd call you home,
He broke our hearts, but made us glad we'd known,
Your mischievous grin, which kept shining through all your pain,
I'm sure we'll never see the like of you again.
You were so full of life, it didn't seem fair,
Everywhere we look we can see you there.
You were so gentle, vulnerable and mild,
Full of courage, for a little child.
We tried to protect you from the hurt you felt inside,
But the dreams we had for you were to be denied.
The legacy you left is hard to follow in its wake,
You gave so much to everyone, and never thought to take.
We're so privileged to have known you at peace with the One above,
We know you're looking down at us, surrounded by God's love.

Spalding

Your soil is fertile, rich and brown,
You are my roots, my hometown.
Standing by the river is beautiful Ayscougfee Hall,
Built in the 1430's therefore a medieval place, I recall.
Famous yew tree walks thought to be 300 years old,
An ancient town, its glory will unfold.
With its busy market, mentioned in the Doomsday Book,
Beautiful churches, well worth a look.
The first Saturday in May,
Has always been the day,
When the famous Flower Parade takes place,
This is when you show your most artistic face.
People come from far and near,
For the most spectacular time of year.
At Christmas time the bells peel out carols that we know,
As we do our shopping we feel that certain glow.
Your bridges strewn with coloured lanterns, that's alright,
To show the way and brighten up the night.
In the spring your fields are covered in flowers,
Stretching as far as the eye can see, with magnetic powers.
Springfield's gardens, Baytree Nurseries, magnificent places to see,
Viewed by millions, featured many times on T.V.
For a small market town, you put on quite a show,
Visitors are amazed, but not locals you know.
We all know the treasure we have here,
As some will discover when they visit next year.

Keep A Candle Burning

Keep a candle burning in your window just for me,
Although I'm far away, I know you'll hope we'll be,
Together very soon, never more to roam,
When my journey's over, then I'll be coming home.
We look at the same moon in the same sky,
Although we're a world apart, you and I,
Our thoughts are entwined through time and space,
I see before me your lovely smiling face.
Distance is no barrier to the memories we share,
Keep the candle burning, then I'll know you care.
The letters we exchanged, we'll keep them every one,
We'll sit by the fire and read them, just for fun.
We'll tie them up again with the same bow of blue,
Put them in a drawer, along with all our memories too.
Every now and then we'll take them out, and stroll down memory lane,
If the going's tough, we'll think about the sweetness that came before the rain.
So keep a candle burning in your window night and day,
It's almost tomorrow, and I'll soon be on my way.

Secrets

I went to this tea dance one Wednesday afternoon,
I saw you smiling at me from across the room.
Suddenly the years vanished and I was once again a young girl,
I felt quite excited, my thoughts were in a whirl.
What if you came over and asked me for a dance?
I couldn't remember how, I was in a trance.
What would I do if you asked to walk me home?
I couldn't ask you in, my secrets would all be blown.
There stood the wig stand, complete with my second wig,
Perhaps it wouldn't bother you, you wouldn't give a fig.
It might be a different matter if you knew I had no hair,
And there's the receptacle for my teeth standing over there.
If I remove my contact lenses, which make my eyes look so blue,
I couldn't even see the room, never mind look at you.
The hearing aid I'm wearing is not easy to see,
If it got switched off accidentally, what a fool I'd seem to be.
I have an artificial leg, though I'm sure you cannot tell,
With my long skirt, it seems to blend in well.
I think I'd better not encourage you to walk across the floor,
My secrets will all be safe I thought, as I left through the
    back door.

Over Sixty

The day I got my pension book, was a milestone in my life,
There's no going back now, no more living on the edge of a knife.
I don't feel any different to what I did a while ago,
Why should I? It's just another day, don't you know.
I can't do all the things at sixty that I did at thirty, it's true,
But my life has moved on to other things, quite interesting too.
Putting pen to paper, letting folks know how I feel,
Enjoying every moment with obvious zeal.
My husband and I are together all the time
No more working in the dust and grime,
We do our shopping at leisure, but still the time will fly,
We sit in a café, drink our coffee, and watch the world go by.
I am profoundly happy that we are still side-by-side,
We sit on a seat and watch the incoming tide.
I never worry about tomorrow, and live for today,
It was different when we were young, we had to make our own way.
Time is what we have, that we didn't have before,
Life has always been fun, and it's never a bore.
With the passing of time, our memories grow sweeter,
Life is more orderly, probably much neater.
It's the only one we've got, so don't let the days grow dull,
We've always known how to live life to the full.

Joe

He was an old man who lived on his own,
Every time we saw him he was always alone.
When he was a young man of only twenty-three,
He was called upon to fight for King and country.
Nothing had prepared him for the trauma that he went through,
And the wounds that he received and still suffers from too.
He had a lovely young wife but that was long ago,
Whenever he talks about her his face has a kind of glow.
His thoughts are forever in the past,
With the things he's loved but couldn't last.
Today's no good you see,
Tomorrow has a kind of uncertainty.
He has lived a lot of years and seen a lot of things,
If only the young would listen and learn from the experience
    that he brings.
He's glad to talk to anyone who wants to hear,
Some folks are glad to be in his company, others turn a deaf ear,
It's their loss, if you know what I mean,
When characters like him are gone and no more to be seen.
He sort of brings history to life, it's better than a book,
All the tales he tells and the steps that he once took.
Be not deceived by an old man whose mind is back in time,
For in his heart he's still young and in his prime.

Sweet Yesterday

Dad would bow, Mum would curtsy, they would dance
    around the room,
They would sing together their own favourite tune.
'I'll walk beside you' rang out loud and clear,
They were oblivious to me standing there.
I can see my mum cycling along the road,
Swaying from side to side with her heavy load.
I remember Dad saying, when I started work,
Do your best in everything, do not shirk,
Save something, even if it's only half a crown every week,
If not, you'll never have any more than your wages, he said
    with tongue in cheek.
I remember asking him one day in 1943,
If the Germans drop a bomb on us, what would become of me?
Then you'd see your mam in heaven, was what he had to say,
Immediately the fear vanished, and just stayed away.
It's just like opening a window in your mind and peering through,
Oh, how sweet was yesterday, such wonderful memories of you.

I Believe

I believe there is a greater power than us on this earth,
We are here for a reason, to learn about our own worth.
I believe our lives are predestined, from way up high,
We can't always see the reason, so ask why.
I believe all life is precious, whether it be animal or mankind,
We should respect others, even if they can't be defined.
If we don't know how to do good, then refrain from doing harm,
To extend the hand of friendship, bring a little peace and calm.
I know this world is a beautiful place, and should be preserved
    for posterity,
I believe in getting the message across, with certain clarity.
I believe in the sanctity of marriage, and am sad when the
    vows are taken lightly,
I believe loyalty is essential, to make your star shine brightly.
Living life to the full in whichever way you choose,
Live and let live, would be my kind of news.
We all have a dream we'd like to achieve,
If we are truly happy, then we've succeeded, I believe.

Peace

Peace is what is needed in this busy life we lead,
To sit amongst the flowers, and take a book to read,
Let quietness overwhelm you, let nature play its part,
Watch the colourful butterflies; let peace fill your heart.
Listen to the buzzing of the giant bumblebee,
Slow down, take time, and you will surely see,
That life was meant to be lived at a slower pace,
Take a look at the viola, and see its funny face.
Have you noticed the ladybirds when the sun is out?
From underneath the leaves they come, they're what
    life's about.
As dusk falls, the aroma of the honeysuckle will fill you
    with delight,
You can spy on the hedgehogs, as they party through
    the night.
If you're very lucky, you might see a badger as well,
All of these wonders could be yours; the secret is not to tell.
So be filled with inspiration, and a quietness too,
This is just the beginning of a whole new life for you.

Woodthorpe Garden Centre

I look forward to my visit to you,
Your cheery greeting rings true.
Once inside, it's a Mecca for folks like me,
Lots of beautiful things to see;
Indoor plants, garden ones as well,
Seeds, bulbs, planters are all to sell.
Sprays and manures in every form,
Tools for everything, including mowing the lawn.
Outside is a lovely pond, near to which is a seat,
Take stock, sit a while, and rest your aching feet.
Have an ice cream, they are sold here,
Greenhouses and sheds over there.
There's an old worldy restaurant, leaded windows and oak beams,
Everything is served, from coffee, to a full meal, it seems.
Through its windows, fluffy goats to view,
Children love it, the scenery is grand too.
There's also a ladies room, if it's needed of course,
How about a garden ornament? Oh look! There's a horse.
We must take some peat and grit,
For now, I think that is it,
We've bought the things that we want, and had a lovely talk,
Just one more thing, in your field we'll take the dog for a walk.

Little Jewels

Little jewels sent from heaven above,
There's no hatred in your heart, you are made from love.
Some of you are white, while others are coffee brown,
The Lord knew what he was doing, when he sent you tiny angels down.
He is asking mankind not to throw his gift away,
That innocents be taught tolerance and kindness, every day.
In the playground, tiny tots hands clasped so tight,
Black and white, catholic and protestant all unite.
God is smiling in His heaven, as he views this scene,
He heaves a sigh; he knows what could have been.
Some of you will encounter racism and fear,
Your creator asks you to turn to Him in prayer.
You are the future of this human race,
So unite now, and put His plan in place.
Sometimes, some of these little jewels are called back home,
We wonder why, maybe the Lord wants them for His own.
Every time a jewel is lost, I'm sure it joins the stars,
And looks down upon this earth, with all its scars.
So treasure these little jewels from far flung lands,
For we are nothing without them, the future is in their hands.

Laughter

Laughter is the chief ingredient of the day,
It gives a lift, and brightens up your way.
It's a tiny miracle we can all perform,
Helping someone to weather the storm.
If your heart is full of laughter, you could make the angels sing,
And watch the merriment and joy that your gift can bring.
The ability to make others laugh is rare indeed,
But just like a tonic to those in need.
Laughter is just as catching as measles or mumps,
It can iron out all your worries, and smooth away your bumps.
To laugh is to be happy, and that's a lovely thing,
So cry little, and laugh a lot and let the rafters ring.

Colours

The world is full of colour, as we all know,
Pink is pretty, and feels warm when the temperature is low.
Lots of people's favourite, cool blue,
Many variations of the same hue.
Always seen at Christmas, hot red,
Like the fluffy slippers by my bed.
Purple, lilac, lemon, cream and brown,
None of these would cause a frown.
God's own colour, in every shade of green,
Hedges, grass and trees all to be seen.
But yellow is my favourite colour of all,
The colour of the sun, that big round ball,
It brightens up the earth, and makes us all warm,
It fills us with happiness, in some shape or form.
Daffodils will add brightness to a dark corner of the room,
Without the gorgeous sun, the world is full of gloom.
Lemon, yellow, gold, call it what you will,
With sunshine and happiness, it does my heart fill.

Isle Of Wight

The first time we saw you, was oh so long ago,
The magic that you held for us is still there, you know.
We've been to other places, it's true,
But there is no comparison with you.
Green leafy lanes, sparkling blue sea,
Home made cakes for tea.
Sandown, Shanklin, the cliff walk,
Quiet places, where people sit and talk.
Osborne House, a wonderful place to be,
Filled with grandeur, and of course history.
Cowes harbour is such a busy place,
Small boats, yachts and ferries show their face.
Blackgang, Saw Mill, I.O.W pearl, the wax works we like very much,
Ventnor we love, the botanical gardens with the tropical touch.
Beautiful Freshwater, Yarmouth, Bembridge, Wootton and majestic Ryde,
Every name conjures up wonderful memories, which fills us with pride.
At night you're just as grand,
Spread out before us, a fairyland.
We view it all from St Boniface Down,
Moving lights of ships that pass Ventnor town.
You have held our hearts for over forty years,
We have come to you, through our laughter or tears.
Tomorrow is not known as we are older now,
But rest assured, we'll get there somehow.

A Walk Along The Sands

As we walked along the water's edge,
Our hearts were light and we made a pledge,
Never again to roam,
And leave our Lincolnshire home.
Sun, sand and glistening sea,
In the distance, the outline of a ghostly ship, with people on board like you and me,
This could easily be a summer's day,
But look at the folks we met on the way.
Scarves, gloves and overcoats were the order of things,
This is the joy that Boxing Day brings.
We don't need anyone to say how lucky we are,
We know of people who can't get very far.
We have a little grumble, but not very much,
We show appreciation for everything we touch.
A day such as this inspires a word,
To one above, we know He has heard.

Alford

Take a walk around Alford and look at what you see,
For every street is steeped in history.
The thatched manor house is a lovely sight to behold,
In its grounds magnificent trees, hundreds of years old.
Step onto the market place, you could be back in time,
With its cobbled streets and stocks, and an atmosphere sublime.
You cannot fail to see the windmill standing so tall,
With its turning sails it seems to beckon to one and all.
A beautiful church stands on an elevated site,
Inviting you to come inside, as perhaps you might.
Dressed in his best regalia is the town crier, an asset to this lovely place,
But for me the crown is its people, presenting a warm friendly face.
There are many more things that I could talk about,
But perhaps you'd like the fun of finding out.

Wealth

They said you were so wealthy, in fact a millionaire,
As I stood there watching you, it was easy to compare,
The clothes you wore, no doubt the best that money could buy,
With the sadness in your eyes, and began to wonder why.
You carry the world on your shoulders, not sure who to trust,
A lonely figure, have all your dreams turned to dust?
I thought of all those happy contented folks I have known,
They haven't any money, but seeds of true happiness they have sown.
They didn't ask for much, but a little more would have been fine,
Taking life as it came, sometimes on the borderline.
I never heard them grumble or say that life is unfair,
But I feel rather sorry for you, standing over there.
Where is the sparkle in your eyes, the joy in your heart?
From your family and friends why did you feel the need to part?
Were you ruthless in your quest for wealth?
Now there's no one to enjoy it but yourself.
But there's no enjoyment, as far as I can see,
Folks are standing here out of curiosity.
What is money for if not to enjoy?
You must have thought this once, when you were a boy.
Where is all the laughter, the joy and the fun?
This is all that matters, when our time on earth is done.
The legacy we leave doesn't have to be money, I might say,
For we are judged on what we are, and not on what we pay.

Masters Of The Sky

A brilliant idea by Barnes Wallis brought 617 squadron
　　into existence,
The faith placed in you, was rewarded by courage and
　　persistence.
Your leader a great warrior, who ranked amongst the best,
But now in a foreign field he lies at rest.
Much was expected of you, it was a time of war,
You did everything asked of you, and more.
The freedom of this nation depended on young men like you,
And with flying colours you came through.
Eight Lancasters and fifty-three crew were lost that night,
Also a black dog called Nigger, whose buried on sight.
Many gallantry awards were won by your courageous deeds,
So with selfless bravery you sowed the seeds,
That others might follow in your wake,
Those split second decisions, that were yours to make.
In those dark filled days, you kept our spirits high,
Many of you were lost, no time to say goodbye.
Fifty years on, the Dambusters are called to war again,
A new generation is experiencing the anguish of parting
　　and pain.

In the Gulf another man's greed has put fear in our hearts,
But we know you are masters of the arts.
No dictator will ever win, while you are flying free,
Whether in Lancasters or Tornados, the proof is there to see.
You were born out of necessity, but became a legend in time,
You've won your place in history, you're still in your prime.
And all those brave young heroes, who started all of this,
To have been a part of it, wouldn't have gone amiss,
But I'm sure they're there in spirit every time you fly,
617 squadron, you were and are masters of the sky.

Retirement

The day that you retired, was special for me,
It meant we could be together more, the way we like to be.
We've spent a lot of years together, though half of it apart,
As work took over, and overruled our hearts.
We always met at night, in the sanctuary we called home,
It was wonderful when we had the time, to pack our bags and just roam.
The holidays we shared, I remember them every one,
They were filled with joy and laughter, and so much fun.
We always had a doggy friend, to share our lives as well,
Teddy is still helping us to weave that magic spell.
Love blossomed in the spring, remember all our dreams,
Spring turned to summer, how we loved our cottage with the oak beams.
Now it's autumn, the years are flying by,
But we are still together, you and I.
We haven't done half the things we planned so long ago,
But that doesn't really matter, the seeds we set still grow.
Now that you are by my side, every night and day,
Perhaps we will fulfil our dreams, as we go on our way.

Our Heroes

They were young and in their prime,
But war was cruel and stole their time.
They must have had their dreams as we all do,
But they couldn't quite make it through.
What were their thoughts, were they afraid?
As with their lives they paid,
They kept our hopes alive when all was doom and gloom,
Their innermost thoughts they took with them to the tomb.
The world is a sadder place for all those young lives lost,
Do we ever stop to think or count the cost?
Freedom demands such a high price,
What would have happened to us if folks like them hadn't
    made the ultimate sacrifice?

Marmalade

Marmalade is a ginger cat, rather big and bold,
One day he got his comeuppance, now it can be told.
We lived near the river, and every day usually just before tea,
A pair of ducks would wander across our lawn, drunkenly,
Now Marmalade would tolerate their presence when there was only two,
But one day they brought along their baby ducklings, and there was quite a few.
Marmalade was fuming, and hid behind the wall,
He didn't see the goose that was accompanying them all,
He sprung out from behind his hiding place, and they all scattered in fright,
But when the goose turned and charged, poor Marmalade panicked all right.
He ran up the apple tree, with the goose gaggling down below,
He sat there trembling; he didn't want the other cats to know,
That he had been outflanked by a goose, who sent him on his way,
Before this happened, he had been king of all he could survey.
But Marmalade learned a lesson, one he didn't care to repeat,
When the goose was about, to beat a hasty retreat.

The Auction

I went into this auction room, wondering what they had in store,
A load of junk I thought, as I walked through the door,
But immediately my attention was focused on this teddy bear,
It was obviously old, with a button in its ear.
It had been loved and treasured once, of that there is no doubt,
If only I could learn its secret, if I could just find out.
How old are you, how many years have you seen?
Were you brand new, when Victoria was queen?
Did the children who played with you then, tuck you up in bed?
All of these questions kept racing through my head.
I tried to imagine what you looked like, all that time ago,
Were you a present for a little girl, whose name we'll never know?
As I stood there pondering all this through,
I heard a voice say, 'it is sold to you.'
I watched in utter silence, as you were taken away,
For you to have stayed with me would have really made my day.
Never mind, there's another auction coming here real soon,
I'll be back again, the same time about noon.

Woodhall Spa

Woodhall Spa is the dream of one man,
A wondrous place, deny it if you can,
Magnificent pine trees, squirrels everywhere,
Rhododendrons the cinema, everything you want is here.
A gorgeous park, swimming pool, tennis courts, bowling green,
Café, lovely flowers to be seen,
A wonderful golf course, and the finest hotels,
A monument to the famous Dambuster's, a story we know so well.
Imagine the railway that came here long ago,
Of all the folks that walked these same streets, that we know,
What a legacy for someone to leave behind,
A tranquil place still, he must have had that in mind.
Standing in the woods looking up at the trees,
It makes us realise how small we are, compared to giants like these.
If you're feeling downhearted, and a little stressed,
Why not come here, to a place that's heaven blessed.

One Lifetime

As a child you could often be seen sitting on the sea wall,
Gazing far out to sea, did you have an inkling at all?
Or did it just happen naturally?
What a remarkable lady you turned out to be,
You played the piano beautifully, your singing sweet and clear,
A ladylike profession, they thought, you had a musical ear,
But you turned your thoughts to other things, and left them mystified,
The years passed, and as a doctor you qualified.
You could have had it easy, staying in your comfortable home,
Oh no, not you, I think you always meant to roam,
To paces no one ever heard of, a mere dot on a map,
Folks laughed, they thought you fell in the crazy trap.
It must have been terrifying for a young girl on her own,
But sheer determination kept you going alone,
It was a dangerous situation, but you came shining through,
A white goddess from another world, that's what they thought of you.
You took on a whole tribe of people, from a different land,
You tendered the sick, and with kindness held out a helping hand.
You learned their language, taught them to read and write,
They learned English, you educated them all right.
You taught them hygiene and of self respect,
Before you came, there was a great deal of neglect.

You won their trust, which wasn't easy I might say,
You faced a lot of opposition along the way,
But gradually your stubbornness proved a winner in the end,
A whole new generation grew up, because you were their friend.
You begged a piano, for the choir that you formed,
Land of Hope and Glory, was what they performed.
You brought them to England, and it was with obvious pride,
They sang beautifully, with you there by their side,
As the world watched and listened, I'm sure they really knew,
They were witnessing a miracle, and all because of you,
But that was only half the story, as I said before,
As a doctor you founded a clinic, right near their own back door.
Thousands of people are grateful, because you conquered the hill of difficulty you had to climb,
And to think you did all of that, in just one lifetime.

Circus

I took Gemma to a circus, and was really quite surprised,
At her reaction to the show, and then I realised,
She was in another world, as I had been all those years ago,
When my parents first took me to see this wonderful show.
The atmosphere was electrifying, when the high wire act was on,
The clowns were hilarious, we laughed till we cried, then in a puff of smoke they were gone.
The horses were magnificent, with their plumes of red,
Waltzing around the ring, a grey horse at the head,
The chimps had a tea party, small dogs jumped through wooden hoops,
The elephants ran around the ring, holding each other's tails,
Then the lion came on, and suddenly silence prevails.
The finale was breathtaking, the glitter of the costumes and the firework display,
Gemma loved it all, and talked about it for many a day.
I had been rather apprehensive in the first place,
I thought it might be out of date, but the look of sheer joy on her face,
Tells me the magic is still there,
The grace, the skill and beauty, that fill the nightly air.

The Driving Test

I bought myself this Lambretta, in a pretty shade of blue,
How to pass my driving test, I hadn't a clue.
I looked at all the books, and learned the Highway Code,
I longed for the day when I could take it on the road,
Without my L plates of course, that is,
I savoured the moment of sheer bliss.
At last the day arrived, when I was to take my test,
I rose early, and would do my very best.
All went well I thought, and then I had this emergency stop, you see,
The examiner said ride around the block until I appear, then stop in front of me.
I rode around the block, but he was nowhere to be seen,
So I went around a few more times, probably thirteen,
Then I went back to the office, where we had started from,
I explained the situation, to a fella whose name was Tom.
After giving me these instructions, the examiner kept writing in his book,
It seems he jumped out into the road, without a second look,
He was hit by another scooter, and taken to hospital straight away,
So my driving test was postponed, for another day.
I had another go, but failed miserably,
As I knocked someone off their bike, while the examiner was watching me.
So I gave up, and sold my scooter to a friend,
She wasn't much better than me, but passed in the end.

Springtime

Spring is the time when all life begins anew,
Young shoots appear everywhere laden with dew.
The days are lengthening, there's more warmth in the sun,
The journey from winter's slumber, has just begun.
The presence of tiny lambs in the fields,
The harvest of wonder, that everyone yields,
There's colour now, where there was bare earth,
This is the season of mirth,
There's an abundance of young birds everywhere,
A kind of magic fills the air,
The trees are full of blossom, Mother Nature wears her finest gown,
Everywhere you look, especially out of town,
There's a feeling of expectation, as spring gets on its way,
The lawns are mown, seeds are sown, they flower where they lay.
Folks have a spring in their step, as they go about their chores,
They smile at others, make new friends, and their heart soars.
This is just the beginning of a brand new year,
Filled with all the things I hold most dear.

Dad

I always thought he would be there,
Sitting in his own armchair,
Reading his paper, listening to the news,
Surrounded by his processions, things that he would use.
The seeds already sown in the trays,
Thinking ahead to warmer days,
In the garden he worked for hours,
Producing veg, fruit and gorgeous flowers.
He was a man of principals, his word was his bond,
He looked for the same trust in others, of which he was so fond.
My mum died when I was a child, during the war,
Part of him died that day too, and was lost for evermore.
The outside world thought he was coping well,
But they didn't know what I knew, and I didn't tell.
Time passed, as time does,
We had a kind of bond, the two of us.
He worked hard, and knew what loyalty means,
For which he was awarded a medal from the Queen.
He was very proud of what he had achieved,
All his life he stood by the principals in which he believed.
I hope I have inherited the same principals I so admired,
He was my dad, and I was so inspired.

Flowers

The earth is full of beauty, but nothing more beautiful than you,
Every colour imaginable, fantastic combinations too,
The elegant snowdrop and the frilled aconite brave the winter's snow,
How they push through the hard ground, I will never know.
Crocus, daffodils and tulips herald in the spring,
The fragrance of the hyacinth, is a truly wondrous thing,
Lily of the valley is a great favourite of mine,
Red-hot pokers like soldiers, seem to stand in line.
Sweet peas are in a hurry to climb to their full height,
Their tiny tendrils entwined around the wire, their perfume fills the night.
The roses, floribundas that stand so tall,
The minute alpines, I love them all.
Look at a black-eyed Susan, its glory will unfold,
Black its eye may be, but the rest is pure gold.
Pansy, peony, iris, to name but a few,
Every one a miracle, they always look brand new.
There are too many to mention, I'm sure you will agree,
But all of them are jewels, so marvellous to see,
Spread out before us, a living carpet out of doors,
I am filled with so much pleasure, and my heart soars.
I just want to work, look and be with them for hours,
So much timeless beauty, when God created flowers.

Your Wedding

I watched you grow up, I'm so pleased to see,
What a beautiful young lady you turned out to be.
Today is very important in your life,
This is the day when you become a wife.
You have the most gorgeous gown to wear,
Just like an angel standing there.
Your bridesmaids dressed in gold and cream,
The colour of your flowers, it's almost a dream.
Your carriage and horses await Madam,
Hurry now, or you will be late for Sam.
Just like a princess in a fairytale,
When you and your prince set sail.
Your parents are there, looking proud and grand,
Hoping everything will go as planned.
The church is full of flowers, and happy people too,
They have come here today, to help make a dream come true.
The organist is softly playing, you will soon be asked to say,
The words that will alter your life, and live a different way.
Some time in the future, when this is a wonderful memory,
Perhaps you will look back and remember that love is the key,
That made all this possible, and wherever you roam,
You will need the key, to turn a house into a home.

There's Always Me

When you need someone to listen, to all the things you want
   to say,
When you feel like walking, or throwing a ball in play,
If you're feeling sorry for yourself, and need some sympathy,
If others don't seem to care, there's always me.
When you need to cuddle up to someone, to let your feelings
   show,
I will say I love you, the only way I know,
I will stand by you, until life's bitter end,
I will always be there, your own faithful friend.
If you're deaf, I will be your ears,
If you're sad, I will share your tears.
If you're blind, I will be your eyes,
When we're together, how time flies.
I want to please you, every way I can,
There's always been this special bond between dog and man.
When your so-called friends have disappointed you,
I will be waiting, faithful through and through.
Sometimes it takes patience to make you see,
In spite of everything, there's always me.

Lincolnshire

It's a magical place, this Lincolnshire I call home,
I've made up my mind to never more roam.
It's difficult to say which is my favourite place,
I am fascinated by your enchanting face,
Land of wide-open spaces where I was born,
A stroll along our golden beach, in the early morn.
The windmills, the wolds, our fertile soil,
Our Lincolnshire folk, and their daily toil.
Somersby where Tennyson once walked the hills,
Lively towns, pretty villages where time has stood still.
From the fens to the sea, I know your worth,
There is no finer place on God's earth.

If

If only I had said the words, that would have made you stay,
But I can't turn back the clock to yesterday,
I was young and rather shy, I didn't know how,
Today I'm much older, and can say it now.
I've been alone, for far too many years,
If I'd known you had too, it would have banished all my fears.
You're just as beautiful to me; I'd have known you anywhere,
The same twinkle in your eyes, and that soft brown hair.
I can see the love in your eyes, that is shining just for me,
So we will start again, the way things were meant to be.
We have a second chance, and I'll not waste it this time,
Although I'm a pensioner now, and some say past my prime,
If that's true, then why this rosy glow,
You and I feel, as hand in hand we go.

My Wish

If I had a wish fulfilled, it would surely be,
To set all impoverished people free,
Free from hunger, want and fear,
To fill their lives with hope and cheer,
To take away all their pain,
And watch them slowly smile again.
To do away with wars and strife,
Just let the people live their life.
Hopelessness is the thought that no one cares,
Let them know that someone hears.
I haven't much to offer, just simple words I know,
But from a tiny acorn, a giant oak will grow.

The Donkey

Children like to ride on his back by the sea,
As he walks up and down, what must his thoughts be?
Perhaps the same now, as in days of old,
When he was part of the greatest story ever told.
In another time, another place,
The Son of God gazed upon his face.
Together they went on their palm-strewn way,
And the little donkey had his day.

A Free Spirit

You were as free as the air you breathed,
Hoping one day, this same freedom to your children could be bequeathed,
But into your world came strangers, who hankered after the things they saw,
You were hounded, intimidated and goaded into war.
You were called savage, by those who didn't really know,
All those who sympathised were called Indian lovers, as history would surely show.
You were backed into a corner, with very little choice,
Death, or submission, you didn't all speak with one voice.
Some of you followed your chiefs to the reservations,
Your descendants are still there today,
But for some the battle ended in the only other way.
You were free spirits who needed to roam those great plains,
The true Native American, so your epitaph remains.
A proud race, great hunters, a people trying to survive,
What would those brave young warriors think, if they could come alive?
You paid the price for trying to stay free,
So your great nation passed into history,
You fought for your independence, to live the way you will,
Many folks since then have died, for this same freedom that is valued still.

Happiness Is

The dawning of a brand new day,
All the folks I've met along the way.
The sun dancing on a glittering sea,
Home made scones for tea.
The look of sheer delight on my two dog's faces,
When a chewy appears from unexpected places.
The majestic trees, the gorgeous flowers,
The beauty of this land of ours.
The sound of a song thrush, hidden from view,
To talk on the telephone with you.
To be able to say what I think, and think what I say,
To live every precious minute of every precious day.
Not to have to work from nine till five,
And the sheer joy of being alive.

Dreams

In my dreams I soar up high,
Like a bird in the sky,
High above the earth below,
I let my imagination flow.
I can see cotton wool clouds, a lot of blue,
A beautiful rainbow, bright shiny hue,
A brilliant orange ball, a pale silvery one near,
Lots of diamonds twinkling everywhere.
I saw the steps to heaven, and the Milky Way,
The golden gate, then quickly turned away.
The picture is fading, and I am turning cold,
I think I'll go back to bed, and put it on hold.

My Wish For You

May you always walk in the sunlight,
With no bad dreams at night,
That you look at the world, through the eyes of a child,
Let your innocence and imagination run wild.
May love endure, your whole life through,
Hope lady luck smiles kindly on you,
And the gold in your heart, be matched by the warmth of
　　your smile,
Your compassion be felt, as you linger awhile.
That friendships and happiness walk hand in hand,
And you can find peace, in a troubled land.

Princess Diana

God looked at all the little people, he'd sent to live on earth,
He was looking for someone special, a being filled with mirth.
He knew the world was lacking something, so decided to lend a hand,
So he created the fairest flower in the land.
Diana was her name, he touched her heart with gold,
And filled it with compassion, for the young and the very old.
The ill, the dying, the very brave, were taken under her wing,
Her smile would light up any room, and make sad hearts sing.
She met kings and presidents, the very rich and the very poor,
She shared a mug of tea with the homeless, and the victims of war.
Millions of people who didn't know her, regarded her as their friend,
She was a beautiful person, the best that God could send,
She was a royal princess, a fairy princess of which little girls dream,
But she had the common touch, which made her quite supreme.
She was a wonderful warm human being, who crossed all barriers to help her fellow man,
Then God thought we'd had her long enough,
So took her back to where it all began.

Charlie

We sat at the breakfast table, Charlie and me,
I saw the note, when I came back with the tea,
It said 'MUM' in large letters on the outside,
I unfolded it, read the words, as Charlie went to the bathroom to hide.
For washing up, one pound,
One pound for taking Toby for a walk,
I don't even stop and talk.
Running errands, one pound fifty pence,
I go twice a day, so it makes sense.
Total three pounds fifty please,
I said not a word, but poured the teas.
Next morning at breakfast, I put a note on Charlie's plate,
Nothing for your clothes I buy, nothing for all the food you ate
Not one penny do I charge for your bike, your computer, not I,
We go on holidays, us three,
I thought we were a family, Toby, you and me.
Total nothing, that's what I wrote,
Charlie read it, and there was never another note.

Bertha

We all look after Bertha, each in our own way,
Who or what is Bertha? I hear you say.
She takes all our attention, all our money too,
Very soon she'll be complete, almost brand spanking shiny new.
Bertha is a Morris eight motorcar, black and red,
They don't make them like this any more, my dad said.
It has a running board, although I don't know why,
It's a marvellous piece of craftsmanship, I'm sure you won't deny.
Her seats are red leather, although there's not much comfort,
    I should say,
But we are infatuated with her anyway.
My job is to polish her, make her shine,
If there's a little smudge the fault is mine.
We pile into Bertha, take her up the road,
Perhaps we could live in her for a week, she could be our abode.
We rode along at thirty, with Dad behind the wheel,
Then along came this road hog, our thunder tried to steal.
'Road hog,' Dad shouted, as he went tearing past,
'That fancy car,' Dad said, 'isn't built to last.'
We go out every Sunday in the summer, heading for the sea,
We pack a picnic basket, and the kettle for a cup of tea.
We look forward to trips out in Bertha, and take care of her
    all week long,
No car was ever loved and treasured more, and she was
    bought for just a song.

Henry

Such a giant of a horse, in every way,
You enjoy your pint of beer, every day,
Such gentle eyes, so trustworthy too,
Such magnificence, when God created you.
Dressed in your finery, on special days,
But free to dream, in other ways,
The sweet taste of hay, the wind in your mane,
The open field beckons, along the country lane.
You pulled the plough, in days gone by,
You've earned your retirement, so say I,
I call your name, you run to greet me,
The moment lingers on, so sweetly.
A grey shire, so glorious to behold,
Humility, strength, trust, gentleness, now your story's told.

Remember Me

Put into practice tomorrow, the dreams we have today,
Do not live in sorrow, because I have gone away.
Go visit the places we both longed to see,
While you are there enjoy yourself, but remember me.
I will be with you in spirit, come what may,
So do not cry for me, live your life today.
I'd hate to see your eyes filled with tears,
After all we had some marvellous years.
I want you to be happy, find someone new,
Do not live alone, I wouldn't want that for you,
You will soon make new friends, you won't be alone for long,
I loved you with a passion, which was so strong.
Live for both of us, but don't be sad,
Remember our life together, and be glad.

Friendship

A friend is someone who stands by you, no matter what it takes,
To help you out when the need arises, and does not hesitate.
Someone to chat to, and tell your secrets to,
But it works both ways you know, if you are there for them they will be there for you.
Friendship is a golden thread shining brightly down the years,
It needs to be treasured, nurtured, or it may disappear.
So if you have a friend you haven't seen for a while,
Show you care, and make them smile,
Sometimes it's all that's needed to lift a heavy heart,
Think of all the joy that you can impart.
I guarantee you will come away, as full of happiness as they,
True friends are few, and lightly scattered,
Let them know they have always mattered.

The Written Word

Without the written word none of us would know,
About the things that have gone on before, how can history show,
The great revelations of another time and place,
Without those faded words on a paper, that give it a human face.
The pen is a mighty weapon, bringing solace to a grieving heart,
Or such laughter, you feel you could easily fall apart.
Some words have a hold on us, they make us feel warm inside,
And fill us with a sense of pride.
I would like to think that a few words I had written,
Would be remembered by someone, after I ceased to be,
Now that's what I call immortality.

The River

It winds its merry way like a silver stream,
Darting in and out, on a patchwork of green,
It passes busy towns with bridges overhead,
Then on into quieter places, where furry creatures have their bed.
Ducks and swans live along its banks,
Other lives have good reason to give thanks.
Cattle are drinking from its cup,
Folks are eating from a basket, they packed up,
Small boats are moored along its edge,
People living near are talking over the hedge.
In places it's full of reeds,
Giving shelter, and fulfilling needs.
Further on folks are fishing, content to sit and while away the time,
At one with their surroundings, and the air that tastes like wine.
Bees buzzing, coloured butterflies everywhere,
A haven of peace, I'm so glad to be here.

Courage

Little acts of courage are played out every day,
Having to face up to things in which you have no say.
Losing someone you love, is a bitter pill to take,
Having to go on, for other people's sake.
Having the courage of your convictions, whatever the consequence,
Standing up for yourself against all odds, is no nonsense,
To admit when you're wrong, if you know it's true,
You'll be a better person, your integrity shines through.
Helping someone else might take great effort on your part,
A feeling of usefulness will surely warm your heart.
To outflank a bully, and send him on his way,
When inside you're all a tremble, and having to pray.
The world loves a winner, as we all know,
But we are all winners as individuals we show,
Our own characteristics in everything we do,
Everything is changing, and we are changing too.
But the old fashioned values that tells us right from wrong,
Are embedded deep within us, and they are really strong.
So each day we find the courage to take a stand,
Against the things we believe are wrong, and should be banned.
These words are for everyone, who thinks their courage may vanish in the light,
If everything you love was threatened, what would you do?
Walk away or fight.

Christmas Time

Christmas is a time of holly and kisses under the mistletoe,
A gathering of loved ones, tall stories in the firelight glow,
Of mince pies, paper hats and coloured chains,
Magical things, where pure excitement reigns.
Parcels wrapped in pretty paper tied with ribbon bows,
Shrieks of laughter from the children, as their frenzy grows,
Singing carols round the Christmas tree,
Reaching out to other lands, across the sea.
Remembering the past, in a nostalgic sort of way,
But meeting the future, as we live from day to day.
A time of giving and warmth, when the weather outside is cold,
The same now, as in days of old,
When it all began with the birth of a baby boy,
Sheltering from the cold, in the warmth of a stable filled with joy.
Gifts were received then, just as they are today,
That's why we celebrate Christmas, in this special way.
The cards we send, with wishes most sincere,
The happiness we feel, knowing people care,
At this time of year, no one should be alone,
Christmas has a special magic, that's all its own.

The Way You Are

You may not be tall and slender, with hair of golden corn,
But God gave you inner beauty, evident from when you
    were born.
This great zest you have for life, just cannot be disguised,
It bubbles up within you, and is mirrored in your eyes.
You extend the hand of friendship to every living thing,
Like the blackbird with the broken wing.
Everyone and everything responds to kindness, of that
    there is no doubt,
Your quiet and gentle ways are well known, no need to
    shout about.
Children run up to you, when they see you in the street,
Other folks wave and smile, if by chance you meet.
You are a great ambassador for the human race,
Nothing is too much trouble, with dignity and grace,
You plough a straight furrow, that always rings true,
Animals and humans alike, all respond to you.
You bring out the best in everyone, you've met so far,
We all love you dearly, just the way you are.

V.E. Day

Victory in Europe, at last the war is over now,
It must never happen again, we must keep that vow.
The greed of one man, that's what it all was for,
We must learn the lesson well, and forevermore.
Nothing was achieved, the price was far too high,
Millions of lives, why did they have to die?
In the darkest hour, when Britain stood alone,
Our spirits were united, true bravery was shown.
Whether you were young or old, rich or poor,
When a bomb fell, there was no discrimination, just war.
The young went in their thousands to defend their native land,
On sea, land and in the sky, they fought the oppressor's hand.
Many young folks perished, some only in their teens,
They died for our freedom, and all the years between.
The survivors were not the same as when they left that day,
Lost in thought for their comrades, buried where they lay.
Now there's been fifty years of freedom, at such a price,
This must still continue, or it will be in vain, their sacrifice.

Picnicking

We all went on a picnic yesterday,
We packed our lunch, and proceeded on our way.
The woods were carpeted with bluebells, odd red campion too,
We saw forget-me-nots, cowslip, just a few.
The trees were tall and slender, reaching for the sky,
We heard the cuckoo, hidden somewhere up high.
Out of the woods along the lane,
Horse chestnuts with flowers like candles, dripping with rain,
The hawthorn, its branches covered in bridal white,
Everywhere we looked, a magnificent sight.
The rain stopped, the sun is shining now,
Time to picnic and ponder how,
This could be so peaceful here,
When it's like a racetrack over there.
We are sitting here, overlooking Alford town,
The fields are now green or gold, where once they were brown.
A white cottage catches our eye, picked out by the sun,
What a lovely place this is, when all is said and done.
We packed our things away, and went for another little stroll,
We watched two horses in a field, then we saw the foal,
All this happened on our picnic one day in May,
When all of nature combined to have its sway.

Thinking Of You

If I had a fiver every time I think of you,
I'd be a millionaire, I'm quite sure that's true.
I'd walk about as if I'm in a trance,
When you were here, I was led a merry dance,
Then one day you left, and I was all alone,
I couldn't believe you'd go, and leave me on my own.
Why did you leave that way?
I will be here if you come home someday.
I am your mum, you're very dear to me,
Perhaps we can work it out, can't we see?
If things were wrong, why didn't you speak out?
I'm always on your side, you surely had no doubt,
I would be here for you, right or wrong,
Come home my son, back where you belong.

Burma Star Heroes

The war was raging close to home, our thoughts were on all of this,
We didn't realise the significance of your plight, and found it easy to dismiss.
It wasn't until later, when the truth finally came out,
That we could comprehend the sheer horror of what it was all about.
Although those of us who stayed at home, can never really know,
Only you who suffered at the hands of such a brutal foe.
Your endurance must have been tested to the limit, in this foul way,
The miracle is, some of you made it home and are alive today,
There has to be survivors to tell of the savagery of other men,
The world listened in disbelief, it has happened again since then.
You unflinchingly gave your all, you had no more to give,
This awful sacrifice of yours, gave us a chance to live.
You fought and conquered the impossible, the victory was won,
Now to rebuild your lives, once the killing's finally done.
War brings out the worst in some, the best in others, it's always been that way,
From heinous acts of violence, to feats of real heroism, what more is there to say?

Band Of Gold

Since you placed this band of gold upon my finger, further back in time than I would care to say,
We've shared the years together, where have they gone? It seems like only yesterday,
We stood before the altar, and made our vows as man and wife,
These vows that we were mindful of, and will keep throughout our life.
We never needed others, it was sufficient that I had you,
The road was sometimes stony, but we helped each other through.
We always did something special, when our anniversary came round,
We wanted folks to know about the happiness we'd found.
There is much to celebrate, in the years that have gone by,
We've always been true to each other, you and I,
I don't understand today's morals, and wonder if they cared,
About the simple pleasures we have, and the love that we have shared.
It's not been all sunshine, oh no, don't get me wrong,
Our troubles have been mere ripples on a stream, put in proportion where they belong.
The magic words for me were, to have and to hold,
Ever since that day, I've worn your precious band of gold.

Puddle Jumper

We had a puddle jumper, an Austin Seven to you,
It was painted all over in airforce blue.
How four of us sat in it, is a mystery to me now,
Along with all our luggage, everything space would allow,
We had some lovely holidays, and trips to the sea,
In our tiny car, we were as happy as could be.
We paddled in the sea, walked in the woods,
We had all we needed, it carried all our goods.
We travelled 25 miles per hour, it didn't matter then,
We had all day, all week to enjoy ourselves, but when,
It became more crowded on the road,
It was more stressful; we needed the Highway Code,
Our halcyon days were nearly over, it would never be the same again,
Our little puddle jumper, who'd taken us out in sun or rain,
Was now becoming obsolete, as Dad shed a silent tear,
But with pride was sporting a brand new shiny motor, and moved up a gear.

Tomorrow

Don't think about tomorrow, or the things we should have done,
Think about today, and having lots of fun,
Remember all the good things, and be glad,
Forget everything that made you mad.
Don't worry about something that can never be,
Just be happy that you were born free,
Free to moan, to walk, to shop, whatever you wish to do,
Take pleasure in the simple things, they are there for you.
You feel the rain, or the warmth of the sun on your face,
You are alive, you can feel, hear and see, so embrace,
Everything that's beautiful, just look around, and feel joy inside,
Take nothing or no one for granted, don't say you never tried,
Self-respect is needed, to help you on your way,
It's not yet tomorrow, remember, it's still today.

Dear Santa

It's almost Christmas time again,
We welcome the relief from the cold and rain.
Soon folks will feel guilty, for a while,
They even look at us, and smile.
Dear Santa, why is it only at Christmas that people care?
What about the rest of the year?
I once lived in a house like you, in the distant past,
I didn't know it would be any other way, it wouldn't last,
Then it's back to my cardboard box, in the cold and dark,
In this great city, I can't even hear a lark.
I don't know if I can face another day,
Perhaps it would be better, if you could take me away.
Have pity on homeless folks everywhere like me,
A bit more Christmas spirit would end our suffering and misery,
So dear Santa, you have a magic spell to weave,
If not, please take me with you when you leave.

G.I. Joe

You came to war torn Britain, from across the sea,
You invaded our lives; my mum even had some of you round for tea.
You were flashy, loud and wealthy, or so it seemed to us,
My sister even married one of you, and there was quite a fuss.
As long as you were happy, Dad said he quite liked him,
But he hoped you'd marry your school friend Tim.
You organised children's parties, took over our village hall,
We danced a different way, thought different thoughts,
We hardly knew ourselves at all.
Just as suddenly as you came, you were gone,
You left a lot of broken hearts, when you moved on,
We didn't know what happened to you, when you left our shore,
But nothing was the same anymore.
It seemed boring to me,
No more G.I.s round our house drinking tea,
No more chewing gum, chocolate bars or cigarettes for Dad,
A telegram arrived, my sister kept crying and was very sad.
You brought colour to our lives, and shook us to our roots,
The war ended, you went home, there were no more G.I.'s marching boots.

Alfred Lord Tennyson

I'd like to talk about Alfred Lord Tennyson, but I'm not sure what to say,
I've seen the memorabilia, Somersby and Bag Enderby churches, and walked the Tennyson way,
I've seen photos of his family, his home on the Isle of Wight,
The statue in the grounds of Lincoln Cathedral, is quite an awesome sight.
His summer home at Mablethorpe is still standing, quite close to the beach,
That vast expanse of golden sands, that is always within reach.
Why oh why did he leave Lincolnshire, when it was such an inspiration, I should like to know,
What happened to his family, are there any descendants, if so,
Do any of them write poetry, perhaps in a different name?
If he could return and walk the hills, he'd find it just the same.
The beauty is still there, for everyone to see,
Looking through a poet's eyes, truly magical it can be.

An Illusive Dream

I had a dream one night, which is still with me today,
It could come true, if only we could meet half way.
The anguish that we feel, must come to an end,
Then maybe once again, we can call each other friend.
Our ways may differ, not easily understood,
But we all belong to the same brotherhood.
Our values may not all be the same,
But if we hurt, we all feel the pain.
If I extend my hand to you, I expect yours in return,
Somewhere along the line, there is a lesson we both must learn.
I burned your house, so you bombed mine,
Now we're both homeless, we both pine,
I killed your son, you took my daughter,
When will it end, this senseless slaughter?
Sometime, somewhere, somehow,
We must find a way to stop it now.
There must be a ray of light, a beam,
This must not remain just a dream.

It's Your Day

Today is very special for you,
Enjoy whatever you want to do,
Buy something you don't really need,
Sit in the garden and read,
Or go for a lovely walk,
Meet friends, stand and talk.
Take a ride on a bus or a train,
Remember this day will not come again.
Put your feet up, make a cup of tea,
Make yourself as idle, or as busy as you want to be.
Celebrate in a way that makes you smile,
It's your birthday, have some 'me' time, for a while.
You're always busy, dashing here and there,
Relax and find some time to spare,
For the important things, that make life worth living,
It's your day, let other people do the giving.

I Know You

I don't know about worldly things, I'm not that wise you see,
But I do know about human nature, folks like you and me.
I know the world is a lonely place, without those you love,
Feelings are so fragile, sometimes you need a kid glove,
To handle the emotions, that swell up inside,
We deny the things that matter, because of pride.
We are fooling no one, trying to tough it out,
I can see right through you, I know what you're about.
That gruff manor is just a disguise you wear,
Hiding a warm and loving heart, beating there.
It was thought manly once, to hide your feelings well,
But the price was too high, if your love you could not tell.
You're not as hard, as you would like us to believe,
Be generous, you'd be surprised at what you could achieve.
Smile as you talk, you'll soon make a friend,
Nothing will seem so bad, in the end.

Maybe

I saw you in a dream, that seemed so real,
Your beautiful house, which had a ghostly feel,
As I walked down your drive, I felt I'd been here before,
The agent said, 'it's only been on the market a week or more.'
Maybe I'd seen it in another life, or time,
I knew something bad had happened here, a heinous crime.
I wanted to leave, but was rooted to the spot,
I had a feeling, you needed me, a lot.
I saw you standing by the window, dressed all in blue,
Our eyes met, but I wasn't afraid of you.
I saw two children, with bobble hats playing in the snow,
Although it was summer, and quite hot you know.
What was it you wanted, I dared to ask?
Only this, just a small task,
Go to the police, and tell them that my husband didn't do what they said,
He wasn't here that night, and I was tucked up in bed,
A noise from the kitchen sent me scuttling down the stairs,
A blow from an iron, sent me crashing into the chairs.
My children need their daddy, please help me if you can,
I've waited so long, to catch the other man.
You'll find him at number 6, just across the way,
Along with my beautiful ring, that he took that day.
Maybe they'd laugh at me, think me mad,
It was just a dream, a dream I had.
I later learned, it was true,
If only I'd believed it too.

You're Always There

I don't need a portrait to remind me of you,
I can still gaze into your hazel eyes so true,
You are always with me, through the day or night,
When the darkness envelops me, you bring me light.
The happiness we knew, is priceless beyond compare,
Until my journey's end, you will be there.
The times we spent together, is a treasure in itself,
I believe I've got the measure of true wealth,
Our life was simple then, no complicated things,
Looking forward to the future, and all it brings.
We couldn't see around the corner, perhaps it was for the best,
That life is gone forever, not at our request.
When things are difficult, and I don't know which way to turn,
I ask myself what you would do, and then I learn.
I can call on you, whenever I feel the need,
In these quiet moments, I let you take the lead.
I draw inspiration from the fact, I knew you well,
I feel you near, when I have something important to tell.
I never feel alone, enriched by the knowledge of your love,
I shall be with you one day, in that happy land above.

Heather Lea

I came here as a bride,
The door to happiness was opened wide,
We were in love, and oh so very young,
No sweeter song than ours, was ever sung.
You were built on a firm foundation, sound and strong,
From the very first moment, we knew this is where we belong.
You sheltered us from the storms, and watched our children grow,
Your rooms were filled with laughter, also tears if we were feeling low.
One by one the children left, we were alone again,
Tucked away down a country lane,
From your top windows we could see forever,
We won't leave here, no never,
Or so we thought, but things are different now,
I have to say goodbye to you somehow.
Everyone has gone, and I'm alone,
I am old, and cannot cope on my own.
The children's ghostly laughter, comes ringing down the years,
My heart is full, as I hold back the tears.
Soon another family will be standing here, instead of me,
They will come to love you too, our home our Heather Lea.

Days Like These

When the world is bathed in sunlight, the sea is very blue,
Anything is possible, your dreams could all come true.
On days like these, the grass is very green,
Your cares are far away, nowhere to be seen.
You come alive, and very much aware,
Of the beauty that surrounds you there.
Flowers, little miracles that spring from this bare earth,
Little treasures, I wonder, do we know their worth?
It's days like these that bird song is doubly sweet,
Little ships on the horizon, where sea and sky both meet.
Tall majestic trees, reaching for the sky,
Dressed in all their beauty, for the human eye.
You wish these balmy days, would never end,
So appreciate everything you see, my friend.

Titanic

You sailed off in a blaze of glory, bands playing a rousing tune,
How could anyone predict the tragedy that was coming your way, so soon?
You bore all the trappings of wealth, for those who could afford to pay,
But the crew, and the not so rich, were also on board that day.
You were on your maiden voyage, all hopes were raised high,
No one would have believed what was about to happen, when they waved goodbye.
You were unsinkable, the whole world knew this was true,
But here you lie beneath the waves, a shadow of the glory that once was you.
Over one thousand lives were lost with you, the world learned with disbelief,
Of the terrible disaster, and was filled with grief.
Now modern technology has allowed us, to see your final resting place,
I was filled with sorrow, for a great ship and all those lives lost,
When fate showed its tragic face.

Dad's Army

I like to watch Dad's Army, it really is a pearl,
Happy memories come flooding back, of when I was a girl.
My dad was in the Home Guard, and had a few tales to tell,
About the blackout, air raid shelter and the church bell.
Three of them guarded the post office all night,
They only had one rifle between them, how could they stand and fight?
But they took their obligations in a serious way,
As Dad's Army is confident to portray.
They manned the lookouts, expecting an invasion on our shore,
Everywhere was as black as could be,
That's why black marketers were about, you see.
One night they heard a lone aircraft, making a strange noise and flying low,
So they piled into the wagon, and followed the sound regardless of friend or foe.
A farmer gave the alert, it had come down in his field,
When they reached the spot, all was revealed.
A body dressed in a German uniform, lay upon the ground,
They searched high and low, but no one else could be found.
The main body of the plane tunnelled under the soil,
Parts of the wings with German markings were visible to all.
Years later, Dad revealed an instant sadness looking at the body of one so young,
He remembers thinking, I suppose you were someone's son.
And that's the way it continued, until hostilities ceased,
The Home Guard was dismantled, the comradeship survived at least.

Together

We met in the pictures one dark winter's night,
I didn't know what you looked like, there wasn't any light.
I don't know why I answered when you spoke, it's a complete
    mystery,
But fate stepped in, and sealed our destiny.
We saw each other in the cold light of day,
I saw your handsome face, and quickly turned away,
I didn't know what you thought of me, and pretended not to care,
I wondered if you liked me, and wished I had something different
    to wear.
You took me to meet your folks at home,
A new life started for me, such as I had never known.
Over forty years have passed since that happy day,
We've had our smiles and tears along the way.
Sometimes we didn't know how we could carry on,
When all those we loved had gone,
But we were there for one another, we helped each other out,
After all, that's what marriage is all about.
I knew you'd take care of me, as best you could,
You have old-fashioned values, that's good.
Your black curly hair is turning grey,
But we still hold hands, in the old familiar way.
We are now in the autumn of our years,
With lots more laughter, and maybe a few more tears,
The fun and laughter have always outweighed the tears and strife,
So we will go on together, until there is no more life.

Alford Craft Market

Walking around the market, I couldn't believe my eyes,
Such beautiful things, expertly made, took me by surprise.
There was a festive atmosphere,
Lots of happy people everywhere,
Jewellery of every colour and kind,
Sparkling glass brought elegance to mind.
Cats, foxes, squirrels, badgers stared at me from this stall,
A full size sheep was being made, it was a marvellous haul.
The paintings were wonderful, especially of Alford windmill and the church,
I saw a tee shirt being hand painted, a parrot on a perch.
I loved the slippers, they reminded me of goblins and fairies and when I was a child,
The pottery was exceptional, the weather dry and mild.
Minerals, dried flowers, woodwork and the cards, things gorgeous to see,
But the rocking horses, mahogany or grey, made me wish I could take one home with me.
All these lovely people demonstrating their skills,
Who said true craftsmanship was obsolete? It's still with us and as old as the hills.
Folks are just as skilful as they ever were, I might say,
So come and watch the expert at work, and have a marvellous day.

Thank You

Thank you Lord for giving me today,
For all the wonderful things, that have come my way,
For the friends I have, and the kindness you have shown,
For the beauty that surrounds me, and the love that I
    have known.
For the good health I have enjoyed, all these years,
For happiness and security, and not too many tears,
For butterflies and birds, whose song is ever sweet,
Without dogs of every shape and size, my world wouldn't
    be complete.
For providing me with warmth, when the weather is cold,
For forgiving all my sins, if I might be so bold,
For giving me the right parents, who taught me right
    from wrong,
For everyone that makes me feel that I belong.
For the talents that I have, whatever they may be,
Thank you Lord for everything, for taking care of me.

The Gurkha

You are a fearless warrior, we're proud to have you on our side,
You fight alongside our troops, and wear your uniform with pride.
Your curved knife, the kukri, is known throughout the world,
Your bravery is saluted, everywhere our flag is unfurled.
Your very name sends a chill to your enemy's heart,
Its range is long, and more lethal than a dart.
You are a proud race, bitter hardships you have known,
When it comes to adversity, great resilience you have shown.
A living legend, whose loyalty has never been in doubt,
A fighting spirit, you know what it's all about.
You're part of a fine tradition, founded in the nineteenth century,
You are unique, your record quite exemplary.
When I hear your name, tunes of glory sound around my ears,
I hope this partnership will continue, for a few more hundred years.

Floristry

Flowers were my business, and had been for many years,
For happiness on many occasions, but sometimes tinged with tears.
I remember a blue teddy bear, for a tiny boy we made,
Although the years have passed, the memories do not fade.
The happiness on someone's face, when a bouquet is delivered to their door,
The wedding flowers caught on a photo that last forevermore.
The baskets of flowers for parents, to say thank you for all that they've done,
The words written on the cards, are second to none.
The holly wreaths at Christmas, with their red ribbon bows,
The pricks we received, the cold in our fingers, that no one knows.
Silver shoes filled with flowers, for an anniversary,
How did the flowers get in there? For some quite a mystery.
Musical cradles for tiny babies new,
Lemon or pink for a little girl, for a little boy was always white or blue.
It's been a wonderful way to spend my working days,
So many friends, so much pleasure, so many words of praise.
The sadness, the frustration, the satisfaction that made us smile,
The people, their stories that made it all worthwhile.

One Moment Of Glory

For over fifty years you kept quiet about the war,
As time went on, folks didn't seem to bother anymore.
It didn't enter our heads what you did in those far off days,
But it gradually came to light, in different ways.
At first you wanted to forget, all that you went through,
As the years passed, you thought no one cared, but you,
Then one day you received this invitation to march along
    London's streets,
In celebration of the forgotten army, and all its feats.
You stood straight and proud, taking your place with the elite,
Your Burma Star shone brightly, your uniform smart and neat.
Young and old alike shook your hand, and patted you on the back,
They wanted to say thank you, for carrying that heavy pack.
You were treated like royalty, everywhere in and out of doors,
For one golden shining moment, the glory was yours.

A Little Thought

It only takes a little thought, on someone's part,
To bring so much happiness, to a sad or lonely heart.
Why not pick up a phone, and ask how they are,
Write a letter or call round, if it's not too far.
If it's a special birthday, and you are far away,
Send a bouquet of flowers; you'll be there in spirit anyway.
That sad and lonely person, couldn't always have been like this,
They must have had another life once, with family and friends, that is.
Ask yourself what would you like, if the positions were reversed,
A caring friend of course, without being coerced.

Funny Man

Children rock with laughter, when they look at you,
Shoes too big, bright red clothes, socks of white and blue,
Curly yellow wig, huge red nose, permanent smile painted on
 your face,
People everywhere will bring their little ones to watch your
 antics, wherever they take place.
But when the show is over, and you remove your smile,
Do you sit and ponder for a while,
About the happiness you bring to people everywhere,
Do they see the man behind the make up, do they really care?
How can they feel the loneliness you endure every day?
All they can see is a funny man at play.
They don't know if you are feeling down,
No one ever looks into the heart of a clown.

Sam

A bundle of fur, and two bright eyes looking into mine,
Was all I see, and then I heard you whine.
I took you home, I had lost my heart to you,
You grew into a beauty, confident, loyal, happy, all of this I knew.
We paced the years together, inseparable you and I,
It's so hard for me now, to have to say goodbye.
We shared our holidays together, paddled in the sea,
You loved it all, your eyes really sparkled at me.
But the years took their toll, and you became so ill,
We tried everything to save you, oh what a gap to fill.
The pain is very real, and just won't go away,
I looked at your empty basket, I think I'll try to fill it today.
So I'm back again, fourteen years along the road,
Looking for a bundle of fur, and two bright eyes, to lift this heavy load.
I can see a kind of miracle taking place,
As another young Sam and I gaze into each other's face.

Barny

Gone missing, a black and white cat,
Won't somebody tell me, where you're at?
Has someone taken you away from me?
Will that someone hear my plea?
I know you wouldn't roam too far away,
I'll say no more, if you're brought back today.
I hope you're not lying injured on the road,
Cats don't know the Highway Code.
How could I cope without you?
Since a tiny kitten, great pals, us two,
I don't want to live alone,
Better ring someone, talk on the phone.
Who can I turn to, in my hour of need?
Oh, where are you Barny? It's time for your feed,
I thought I heard a faint meow, maybe it's in my head,
I remember now, better fetch my neighbour Fred,
He went up into the loft, as he had done two days ago,
He had my beloved Barny, and was coming down real slow.

The Lone Sailors

You undertook the vast adventure on your own,
Whatever came your way, was met by you alone.
Most of us just sit and dream, from the comfort of our armchair,
Oh no not you, the dream was reality, you were there.
You journeyed into the unknown, the unpredictability of it all,
Failure was never on your mind, the spirit of adventure was standing tall.
At times the weather was atrocious, a small boat tossed by a gigantic sea,
As you fought this battle completely alone, did doubts creep in, or did you think what will be will be?
Some of you came home in glory, waiting crowds cheering you on your way,
While others slipped into the harbour, unseen at the break of day.
You all accomplished a dream, which is a wonder in itself,
None of you would have traded in that dream, for someone else's wealth.
One lone sailor pitted against the elements, as nature did intend,
How could anyone doubt your courage? That won through in the end.

Thoughts Of You

Images of you are always on my mind,
You were so gentle and kind,
We asked why you had to go,
But it wasn't for us to know.
You lived a life that wasn't very long,
But your will to live was so strong,
Your laughter was as infectious as a bright sunlit day,
Touching everyone you met, as you went on your way.
You were as a bright butterfly that lived only for a while,
But oh how I remember that gorgeous smile.
When a light is extinguished there's blackness everywhere,
Gradually our eyes become accustomed, and we see other folks there.
We know we're not alone, in the sadness that we feel,
With the passing of time, our broken hearts will heal.
I think of you often, and the happiness that radiated from you,
And count myself lucky, and privileged to have known a heart so true.

My Beloved Husband

You would know the agony I am going through,
If the roles were reversed, it would be the same for you.
I am lost, afraid, lonely and cold,
No comforting hand to hold.
Gone is the laughter, that devastating smile,
The surprises you sprung, once in a while.
I have a treasure chest of memories to recall,
One day maybe, I'll lift the lid and not cry at all.
You were the one, who opened up the door,
You were all I wanted, and more.
When times were hard, your arm was firm and strong,
I now need your courage to go on.
You fought bravely, right until the end,
You were my husband, my lover and my friend.

ADMISSION 6d

Admission 6d, that's what the notice said,
I was going to the shops, but I'll go in here instead.
I don't know what it's all about,
If I don't like it, I can always walk out.
I saw marrows that would satisfy a giant,
Tall roses beautiful, aloof and defiant,
Jars of homemade jam, standing in rows,
Pickles, cakes, wines that would curl your toes.
A stall full of garden gnomes, made me smile,
I liked the one with the fishing rod, so lingered awhile.
Massive pumpkins, I expected Cinderella to appear,
Oh, how pleased I am, that I walked in here.
Huge vegetables, some of which I'd never seen before,
I meant to take something home, when I walked out the door.
Pots of multicoloured flowers, kept beckoning to me,
But I bought a wheelbarrow filled with pansies, then went
    for a cup of tea.
As I enjoyed the fruit cake,
I wondered what else I could take.
I settled for a gardening book, to tell me how and when,
Fifty years on I still refer to my book, now and then.

A Little Dog Called Jack

He came to us in the spring,
He was such a tiny thing,
We loved him, and fussed over him, and watched him grow,
How much we miss him, he will never know.
He loved to run in the woods, paddle in the sea,
On holiday, he even shared a lilo with me.
At Christmas there was always presents for him, as well as us,
How his eyes would shine at all that fuss.
Hanging bonios on the Christmas tree,
Disguising them with tinsel, so he couldn't see.
He always told us when the phone was ringing, the doorbell too,
All these things I remember, when I think of you.
The wagging tail, when family or friends called round,
The juicy bones you took down the garden, and buried in the ground.
You used to help dig the garden, but not always in the right place,
The sheer joy of living was stamped upon your eager face.
You gave more to us, than you can ever know,
Your journey over, we had to let you go.
I'd have given everything I owned, to have him back,
My little dog called Jack.

Politics

You might think politics a bore,
But what about the folks who's gone before?
Who fought so bravely for our right, to have our say,
So think about their anguish, and cast your vote today.
You might think them all the same,
And you'll not go along with their little game,
But remember if you want to change the way things are,
You must raise your voice, put yourself on a par,
With the millions who have this special right,
Think of what you want, and maybe you just might,
Tip the balance in your favour, the things you want to see,
It's up to us to change the things, with which we don't agree.
It's no use saying afterwards, what am I going to do?
I'll tell you now, put your cross against the name that
    represents your point of view.

James' Mouse

It was a lovely day, our door was open wide,
Pam was making tea, when suddenly she espied,
Something tiny running across the kitchen floor,
I thought she was being murdered, as she screamed and banged the door.
I was threatened with divorce, if I didn't catch it there and then,
So I set about the task, so peace could reign again,
And then we drank our tea, and watched Jamie our neighbour's little boy,
Playing in the garden with some toys.
We strolled into the garden, and was asked by Jamie's dad,
'Have you seen Pepper, Jamie's mouse?' We said we hadn't, but wished we had.
It seemed Pepper had vanished from their house,
And I had annihilated Jamie's pet mouse.

The Flower Fairy

Tricia and Becky were friends, and played together all the time,
They had a secret hideaway, with only three steps to climb.
One day they heard singing very faint, they followed the sound,
They couldn't believe their eyes, there sat this fairy on a grassy mound.
She stopped singing when she saw them, hello, she said, my name is Pansy, who are you?
I'm Becky and I'm Tricia, the girls said, feeling shy, not knowing what to do.
Would you help me onto that toadstool, said Pansy with a smile,
I think I'll brush my hair, and stay for a while.
Her hair was long and golden, and shone in the sun,
Her tiny wings were transparent, her dress both green and blue in one.
I'm called Pansy she said, because I'm a flower fairy you see,
They didn't really, but nodded their heads to agree.
Are you thirsty? Becky asked, Pansy replied just a bit,
I'll fetch a cup from our doll's house, with some lemonade in it.
Pansy said I always drink the morning dew, so this is a treat,
Becky replied I ought to have brought you something to eat.
Just then Tricia's mother called out, it was time for tea,
Let's bring it out here, and picnic under the tree.
They vowed to keep the secret, and their fairy friend,
Next day they ran to their hideout, a message they tried to send.

But everything had vanished, Pansy, the toadstool, the mound all
   except the tiny cup,
So it was all real said Becky, as she stooped to pick it up.
Tricia felt something brush against her face, and heard a tiny
   voice say,
Don't you know my dears, that yesterday was Midsummer's Day.

Martha's Birthday

Today Martha is 100 years old,
We've listened spellbound to the stories she has told;
The Boer war was raging in a far off land,
Victoria was still queen, it was Oscar Wilde's last stand.
Lillie Langtry performed on stage,
The cakewalk, an American dance, was all the rage.
The Labour Party was born, with Ramsey Macdonald at the helm,
Marconi spans Atlantic with wireless message, Royal Navy is
 overwhelmed.
Carriages go without horses, giant liners race across the sea,
Flimsy planes take to the skies, and Martha ate newly made
 scones for tea.
Captain Scott and his companions, perished in the snow,
Mary Pickford came to the silver screen,
Lawrence of Arabia rode his camel to victory, if you know what
 I mean.
R34 Airship was still around when,
Martha worked for a living downstairs then,
As she went about her duties, in this grand house,
Her employers hardly noticed her, quiet as a mouse.
In 1921 Enrico Caruso died, which made Martha very sad,
That same year she went to the seaside, and felt very glad.
She saw man's inhumanity to man, in two world wars,
She bobbed her hair, and danced the Charleston, of course.
She laughed at Charlie Chaplin, like people everywhere,

The death of Valentino, filled her with despair.
She felt humbled by a king, who gave up all for love,
And bought herself a bird of peace, a little white dove.
The time machine by H.G.Wells was as outrageous as going
　　to the moon,
She never thought that would happen, let alone so soon.
Martha has now flown the Atlantic, which surpassed her
　　wildest dreams,
That she should have lived to see all that is a miracle to
　　everyone it seems.

Shed No Tears For Me

If you are reading this, then I have ceased to be,
So be not sad, and shed no tears for me.
I have grown up and old, since I have joined the war,
The freedom we took for granted, has never been valued more.
I don't know this man, this enemy I'm fighting and can't tolerate,
All that he stands for, so I must learn to hate,
This unseen human being, that comes hurtling at me from the sky,
When I'm in my aeroplane, I do the same to him from way up high.
Many friends have come and gone, fighting this ruthless foe,
But it has to be worth it, for all those dear familiar things we know.
Tyranny must never get the upper hand,
We will fight and maybe die, defending this fair land.
So dear Mum, I'm writing this little poem,
Hoping you will never read it, and I'll be coming home,
Your letters are so real, and keep me sane inside,
But beneath the lines, I sense the fears you hide.
Don't make me out to be a hero, for I'm not very brave,
I tremble at the oncoming battle, but am more terrified of being
     a slave.
Tell Auntie Mable I love her, and of course Dad and you too,
I know about the bombing and the trauma you're going through.
If you are reading this, then do not weep,
For I am not gone, but merely asleep.
I have lived in the sunlight, flown in the clouds,
Crammed in twenty years one lifetime, but no shrouds
For me, as I keep up the pace,
I will take God's hand, and feel His warm embrace.

Ever The Optimist

Today is yesterday's tomorrow,
Waste not your time, it's only yours to borrow,
Peer through the dark clouds, and see the silver lining,
Somewhere, sometime, your sun will be shining.
Wake up every morning, with hope in your heart,
Do something different, and make it part,
Of this rich pattern, known as life, weave a colourful spell,
Filled with dreams, happiness, friendship and make it tell.
Follow your star, wherever it may lead,
Never give up, or you'll be the one in need,
Walk a different way, see a different view,
Something wonderful could be waiting there for you.
Stretch out your hand to someone, who may need a firm hand to hold,
The pleasure and satisfaction, your whole being will enfold,
Fill your life with interest, of one kind or another,
Don't waste your time, for there won't be any other.
Don't sit and think, what might have been,
Go and live life now, and let yourself be seen.